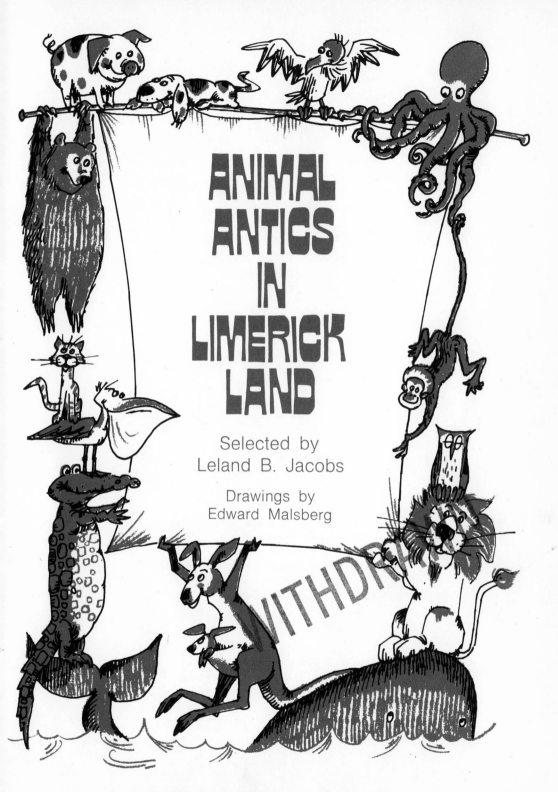

# ANIMAL ANTICS IN LIMERICK LAND

Selected by
Leland B. Jacobs

Drawings by
Edward Malsberg

**GARRARD PUBLISHING COMPANY**
CHAMPAIGN, ILLINOIS

## A NOTE TO THE READER

This book includes "classic" limericks from such great writers as Edward Lear and Oliver Herford. In addition, it contains a large number of unsigned rhymes. No collection would be truly representative without the work of these "unknowns" who have done most of our limerick making.

The editor and publisher acknowledge with thanks permission received to reprint the limericks in this collection.

Acknowledgments and formal notices of copyright for all material under copyright appear on page 62 which is hereby made an extension of the copyright page.

# Contents

# There Was an Animal Small

## Puppy Problem

A puppy whose hair was so flowing
There really was no way of knowing
    Which end was his head,
    Once stopped me and said,
"Please, sir, am I coming or going?"

*Oliver Herford*

## Cat Food

Our kitten—we all call him Huey—
Will never eat liver so chewy,
    Nor the milk, nor the fish
    That we put in his dish.
He only will dine on chop suey.

## Half Happy

A worm in an apple, they say,
Was ever so happy that way
    Till a fellow named Dapple
    Bit into the apple...
The worm was half happy that day.

*Lee Blair*

## Fined

Said the snail to the tortoise: "You may
Find it hard to believe what I say;
    You will think it absurd
    But I give you my word
They fined me for speeding today."

"Well, well!" said the tortoise. "Dear me!
How defective your motor must be!
    Though I speed every day,
    Not a fine do I pay:
The police cannot catch me, you see."

*Oliver Herford*

# Sky-High

A grasshopper hopped in the square.
It hopped on a girl sitting there.
   It chirped in her ear,
   Which filled her with fear
And sent her sky-high in the air.

*Lee Blair*

# Rabbits from Carden

Some rabbits came over from Carden
And ate up most of my garden.
    They feasted for hours
      On stalks and on flowers,
And never once said, "Beg your pardon."


# The Hungry Moth

That moth—the hungriest bug—
Nibbled Grandma's wool dress, with a shrug,
    And Grandfather's hat—
    And then after that,
He ate a big hole in their rug.

*Merlin Millet*

# P. U.

Though I'm passing the word on to you,
I am not sure that it's true:
    Some people of knowledge
    Say skunks have a college
That goes by the name of P.U.

*Lee Blair*

## Skunks' Way

In the woods on a fine autumn day,
A hunter met skunks on his way.
   Cried little skunks three,
    "A gun we can see!"
And mother skunk said, "Let us spray."

# So Many Monkeys

Monkey Monkey Moo!
Shall we buy a few?
    Yellow monkeys,
    Purple monkeys,
Monkeys red and blue.

Be a monkey, do!
Who's a monkey, who?
    He's a monkey,
    She's a monkey,
You're a monkey, too!

*Marion Edey*
*and Dorothy Grider*

## That Bird

A bird sitting up in a tree
Was not singing "chirp" or "chee, chee."
   That bird on the bough
    Was singing "meow,"
Because it's a catbird, you see.

*B. J. Lee*

## What the Owl Said

An owl, at the morning's first ray,
Flew off, and in going did say,
   "In the woods dark and deep,
    I'll settle and sleep,
For I don't give a hoot for the day."

## What the Condor Said

Said the condor, in tones of despair:
"Not even the atmosphere's rare.
    Since man took to flying,
    It's really *too* trying,
The people one meets in the air."

*Oliver Herford*

# Parrot Talk

A parrot from old Trinidad,
When ruffled, or angry, or mad,
   Gave out a loud squawk
   And started to talk
Polly—syllabically bad.

*B. J. Lee*

## Stung

There once was a boy from Obad,
An inquisitive sort of a lad.
    He said, "I will see
    If a sting has a bee."
And he very soon found that it had!

*Jay Lee*

# An Odd One

There once was a finicky ocelot
Who all the year round was cross a lot
    Except at Thanksgiving
    When he enjoyed living
For he liked to eat cranberry sauce a lot.

*Eve Merriam*

# At Thanksgiving Time

A handsome young turkey, they say,
In November went dashing away.
    The reason the bird
    Took off is he heard
The plans for his Thanksgiving Day.

*B. J. Lee*

# There Was an Animal Tall

## Full Meal

When dining, a Nanny Goat said,
"Don't bring me the salad and bread.
   For what I like best
   Is a bit of wool vest,
And a shirt, and a tie that is red."

*Lee Blair*

## Lonely Cow

An Alaskan cow, new at the zoo,
Was ever so homesick and blue,
    Since no other cow
    Round about there knew how
To respond to her best Eskimoo.

                    *B. J. Lee*


## The Gnu Knew

An inquisitive lady from Kew
Said, when she got to the zoo,
    "My word! Is it true
    That *that* is a gnu?"
Now she knew. And the gnu knew it too.

## To and Fro

A cheerful old bear at the zoo
Could always find something to do.
    When it bored him to go
    On a walk to and fro,
He'd reverse it and go fro and to.

## Hibernation

When in winter it snows and it snows,
A bear slumbers snug in repose.
   Though humans may doze,
    When it snows and it snows,
It's the bear knows repose, I propose.

*Merlin Millet*

# Polar Bear Talk

Polar bears gleefully walk
Where the snowfields are whiter than chalk.
    They find it is nice
    To nap on the ice,
And they use icy tones when they talk.

*Lee Blair*

From . . . . .
# Dragon

A Dragon named Ernest Belflour
Who lived in a dark palace tower
    Played an old violin
    Of dried-out sharkskin
Hour after hour after hour.

An Indian Princess one day,
Who happened to wander that way,
    Said, "The sound of that thin
    Dried-out violin
Has stolen my heart away."

So she climbed the steps of the tower
And there beheld Ernest Belflour,
    Who was changed by her glance
    To a handsome young Prince:
She had broken the Old Witch's power.

They were married the very next minute
By a neighbor, Sir Larchmont of Linnet,
    And they danced to a thin
    Dried-out violin
Accompanied by a very shrill spinet.

*William Jay Smith*

# What the Camel Said

If all of your life you were humpy
And swayed over sand, lank and lumpy,
    You'd probably be
    Exactly like me—
Though perhaps you'd be even more grumpy.

# Laughing Hyena

A hyena, cultured and bright,
Sat and read by the moon's lovely light.
    The limericks he read
    So tickled his head
That he laughed through the whole of the night.

*B. J. Lee*

## A Weighty Problem

An elephant, looking dismayed,
Cried out, "I am really afraid
    I'm getting too fat."
    And having thought that,
The elephant promptly got weighed.

# An Elephant

An elephant sat on some kegs,
And juggled glass bottles and eggs,
    And he said, "I surmise
    This occasions surprise,—
But, oh dear, how it tires one's legs!"

*Joseph G. Francis*

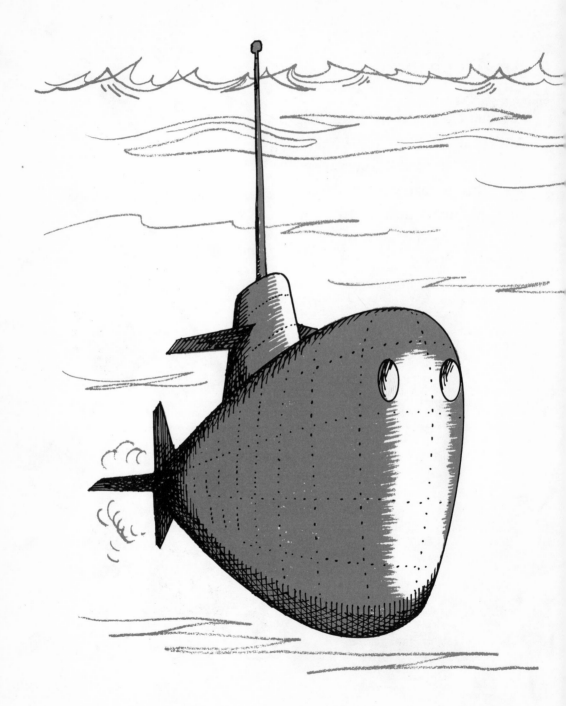

# There Was a Creature of the Sea

## What Was It?

The first time a young sardine
Got a view of a big submarine,
    Mamma Sardine said,
    "Now don't be afraid.
That's a can full of people you've seen."

*Lee Blair*

## Dismay

A turtle went sadly away
In horror and fear and dismay
   When he read on a sign
   Where gentlemen dine,
"Enjoy turtle soup here today."

*Lee Blair*

# Terribly Blue

An oyster wept, "What shall I do?
I'm feeling so terribly blue,
    For it's my assumption,
    As well as presumption,
I'm sure to end up in a stew!"

# Fishes' Wishes

I've inquired of all kinds of fishes
About their great hopes and their wishes.
    Whether carp, cod, or trout,
    They all want to stay out
Of nets, and skillets, and dishes.

*B. J. Lee*

# Pelican

An unusual bird is the pelican.
Can he waddle and swim? You can tellican!
    And can he eat fishes—
    So fresh and delicious?
If you watch, you will know very wellican.

*Lee Blair*

# Man-Eating Shark

A lady swimmer from Sark
Met up with a *man*-eating shark.
   The shark swam away
   From the lady that day,
And she safely swam home before dark.

*Anonymous*

# The Fish-ish-ish

Deep in the woods, in a brook-ook-ook,
In a pool, beside a nook-ook-ook,
    A fish I caught
    And promptly brought
It home to give to Cook-ook-ook.

I said, "My pole and hook-ook-ook
Down to the pool I took-ook-ook,
    And here's my prize."
    To my surprise,
"It's rather small," said Cook-ook-ook.

When I heard that, I shook-ook-ook
My head and said to Cook-ook-ook,
　　"It may be small,
　　But after all
Who catches whales in a brook-ook-ook?"

　　　　　　　　　　*B. J. Lee*

## To Sea on a Goose

There was an old man of Dunluse
Who went out to sea on a goose.
    When he'd gone out a mile,
    He observed with a smile,
"It's time to return to Dunluse."

*Edward Lear*

# Crocodile Ride

One summer day, with a big broad smile,
Lyle rode on the back of a crocodile.
    He called out to say,
    "Here's the very best way
To go for a daredevil ride on the Nile."

*B. J. Lee*

## Envy

Oh, how I envy the whale!
He can weather the stoutest of gale,
 And whatever the tide,
 He knows how to ride,
With neither a rudder nor sail.

# Whale

When I swam under water I saw a Blue Whale
Sharing the fish from his dinner pail,
 In an undersea park
 With two Turtles, a Shark,
An Eel, a Squid, and a giant Snail.

When dinner was over, I saw the Blue Whale
Pick up his guests in his dinner pail,
 And swim through the park
 With two Turtles, a Shark,
An Eel, a Squid, and a giant Snail.

*William Jay Smith*

# On April First

An octopus sat on a stool
While a haddock and shark played at pool.
 "That's all very odd,"
 Said a whale to a cod,
"So I think it must be April Fool."

*Elbee Jay*

# Do Not

Don't try to tease that crocodile,
Or try to please that crocodile,
    Don't prod or poke
    Or try to stroke,
Lest he should seize—that crocodile.

# Why That Smile?

There was a young lad from Decatur
Who would not take advice from his pater,
   Nor his mater—and so
   To a swamp he did go.
Why that smile, you sly alligator?

*B. J. Lee*

# There Was This Animal Too

## His Reason

An ant to a lion said, "Why
Do you keep looking up at the sky?"
    Said the lion, "The rain
    Takes the curl from my mane,
And there's not a beautician nearby."

*B. J. Lee*

# The Chase

Higgery, diggery, dig,
My mother was chasing the pig
    Up one street and down
    All over the town,
Because he was wearing her wig.

*Elbee Jay*

# Higglety, Pigglety

Higglety, pigglety, pop!
The dog has eaten the mop;
The pig's in a hurry,
The cat's in a flurry,
Higglety, pigglety, pop!

*Samuel Goodrich*

## The Ichthyosaurus

There once was an ichthyosaurus
Who lived when the earth was all porous.
 But he fainted with shame
 When he first heard his name,
And departed a long time before us.

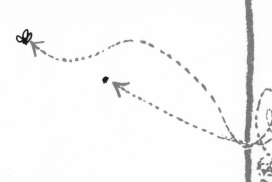

# The Flea and the Fly

A flea and a fly in a flu
Were imprisoned, so what could they do?
    Said the fly, "Let us flee."
    "Let us fly," said the flea.
So they flew through a flaw in the flu.

## Lost and Found

Little Bo Peep has gone 'round
To hunt for her sheep. I'll be bound,
    Somewhere they must be.
    If I had been she,
I'd have gone to the school's "Lost and Found."

## Not Sleepy

When in bed I'm not very sleepish,
I count sheep, all the while feeling sheepish.
    I count up to ten
    Again and again
Till the whole situation's Bo-Peepish.

# The Kangaroo

It is a curious thing that you
Don't wish to be a kangaroo,
    To hop hop hop
    And never stop
The whole day long and the whole night too!

*Elizabeth Coatsworth*

## Misfortune

There was a young man named Fall
Who went to a fancy dress ball.
   He went, just for fun,
   Dressed up as a bun,
And a dog ate him up in the hall.

# The Animal Fair

I went to the animal fair.
The birds and the beasts were there.
   An old baboon
    By the light of the moon
Was combing his auburn hair.

*Old Rhyme*

# Might and Mane

A handsome young noble from Spain
Met a lion one day in the rain.
　　He ran in a fright
　　With all of his might,
But the lion, he ran with his mane!

## Absentminded

How absentminded was Wister!
He went walking one day with his sister.
    A cow, with its horns,
      Tossed her into some thorns,
And poor Wister—he still hasn't missed her.

# Acknowledgments

Atlantic-Little, Brown and Co.: For "Dragon" (20 lines) and "Whale" (10 lines) from *Boy Blue's Book of Beasts* by William Jay Smith, by permission of Atlantic-Little, Brown and Co. Copyright © 1956, 1957, by William Jay Smith.

The Macmillan Company: For "The Kangaroo"—15 lines from *Summer Green* by Elizabeth Coatsworth. Copyright 1948 by The Macmillan Company. Reprinted with permission of The Macmillan Company.

Charles Scribner's Sons: For "So Many Monkeys" from *Open the Door* by Marion Edey and Dorothy Grider. Copyright 1949 Marion Edey and Dorothy Grider. Reprinted by permission of Charles Scribner's Sons.

# Index of Authors